Breaking Free

Poems of Nature, Soul & Liberation

Harshita Singh

BookLeaf
Publishing

India | USA | UK

Made with ❤ on the BookLeaf Publishing Platform
www.bookleafpub.in
www.bookleafpub.com

Dedication

To the souls yearning to break free, to the hearts seeking their own rhythm, and to the winds that carry dreams beyond boundaries—this is for you.

Preface

We are all bound in some way—by time, by expectations,
by memories that refuse to fade. But just as the river
carves its path through stone, just as the wind defies the
weight of gravity, we, too, are meant to break free.
This collection is a tribute to that journey—the struggle,
the surrender, the awakening. Through the changing
seasons, both in nature and within our hearts, these
poems capture the essence of letting go, embracing the
unknown, and finding solace in the wild, untamed
beauty of life.
"Breaking Free" is not just about escape; it is about
rediscovering ourselves beyond the limits we once
believed in. I hope these words resonate with you,
echoing the whispers of the wind, the rustling leaves,
and the silent courage of the stars.
Welcome to this journey of liberation.

With gratitude,
Harshita Singh

Acknowledgements

This book would not have been possible without the love, support, and inspiration I have received along the way.

First and foremost, I extend my deepest gratitude to **my mother, my lovely sister and my love**, who have encouraged me to embrace my love for poetry and given me the strength to bring this collection to life. Your belief in my words has been my greatest motivation.

A heartfelt thank you to **my dearest friends** for instilling in me a passion for storytelling and the beauty of language.

To nature itself—the ever-changing seasons, the whispering winds, the quiet snowfall, the golden sunsets—thank you for being my muse and filling my heart with endless wonder.

Lastly, to **my readers**—whether you stumbled upon these pages by chance or sought them out intentionally—thank you. Your presence gives these words meaning, and I hope they find a place in your heart, just as they have in mine.

With gratitude,
Harshita Singh

1. Un-learner- The learner on an unlearning process!

The **Un-learner** in me is ready to **set free**,
Let loose all the binding miseries,
I have been told a hundred times about things that
matter
But they mattered to me not even once
So, I shook my head in denial, as their ego shatter
I do so whenever I get the chance.

It took me years to unlearn things what has been sold to
me like
Oxygen to our lungs
How important it is to show what you own
This false idea of the world I completely disown

I have my own thoughts to unlearn for a while
And I am working on unlearning a lot of things with a
broad smile

Yes I am a **un-learner** and it took a lot of guts to reach
this place
I am in no hurry as for me, this is my life
Not your modern world race.

2. Honesty- a shame to the shameless!

Am I too honest for this world?
They said I have no guilt for what I say
As If my mouth has no control or brake
But I feel it is connected to my innermost organ
Called heart,
Yes I got no shame for a naïve to start
To speak up for the matters that I truly believe in
If you think I am shameless for doing so,
Let it be, because I am not here to win
But to broaden, your perceptions of reality
That has been distorted

I won't sugarcoat my words for your convenience
If you want that,
Please find one with mere lenience.
To face me is like facing the death in the eye,
You know it is coming for you, still you want to be alive.

Being honest, comes with tags of being shameless too!
And I gladly accept it.

3. A maximalist- How much is too much?

I am a **collector**,
I want this, I want that,
Because I saw it somewhere in the ad

For the society only then I will be at par,
But those things are away from my sight of use so far.

I will have pairs of shoes, some of which I don't even
wear
But who cares about that kid in the street walking
barefoot
I am not the one to choose to bring any change
In his life for a good

I have to show everyone how much I own,
Because it is taught in my society as something to brag
upon

Who says money doesn't buy you happiness?
I can prove you wrong by finding new things to chase
I can fill that void and can refill it with every new
purchase

I have been taught to value materials more than human
being
After all, I can **use humans and love all other things**.

4. Chasing- A world worth living?

I've spent my life chasing.
That's what I was taught from the start—
Only if you chase, will you receive.

At school, I chased good marks,
Hoping for a future that would shine.
In college, I chased placements,
Craving the thrill of accomplishment.
At work, I chased promotions,
Clocking in hours beyond reason—
While slowly forgetting how to care
For my own mind and body.
But now, looking back,
I see I've lived half a life I never truly enjoyed.
Just running in circles,
Inside a never-ending maze.

And somewhere along the way,
In silence, in reflection, I arrived at this truth:
I no longer want to chase.
Not success.
Not perfection.
Not even a person.

Now, I want to live the other half of my life—
With love,
With care,
With joy and quiet excitement.
And yes, with sorrow and pain too.
I want to embrace detachment,
Learn to breathe in a carefree way.
I want to stop running.
I want to *feel.*
To spend more time living
And less time proving.
To choose presence over pressure.
And peace over pursuit.

I think that's what I'm going to do.
And I think that's what I'll be good at.

5. This life- a heaven or hell?

Being in my early thirties,
I think I've tasted life long enough
To tell you a little about it.
I feel for those who aren't able to enjoy it—
Held back by lack of resources,
Or the absence of a man they hoped would complete
them.
They call it *hell*,
Trapped in their shells,
Looping through loneliness.
And honestly,
It's not their fault.

We were conditioned this way.
I feel for myself, too—
When I witness those who have little
Yet give everything they can.
They've built a heaven
Out of kindness and grace.
They may appear ordinary,
But their hearts burn like a thousand suns.
They don't curse life—
They warm it.

And me?
I think I'm somewhere in between
Heaven and hell.

Because I've walked through both.
I've known joy that opens the soul
And pain that folds it shut.
I've been a receiver.
And I've learned how to give.
Maybe that's the point—
Life gives, and life takes.
It slays and soothes,
In a single breath,
Every day.

6. The realm-beyond the clouds

They say they have got vision,
But all they do is they see what
Their eyes can show.
Their limit is the sky but not beyond the Clouds
And they hate to hear this when I say

There is a realm, that exist
Beyond those thick bushy clouds
That does not decides on right or wrong
That uncovers itself only after heavy rains
That realm is the vision one should aim for.

So, before you decide on the things that make your heart
heavy
You should visit that realm once
But make sure not to get caught up there
Because it is warm and cozy,
Life on the surface is not that rosy.

Extend your vision beyond those clouds
And you will be born once again.

7. Eyes-gateway to the heaven

When your eyes collide with mine, you must know
I can see your soul too
You can hide yourself from that mouth but
Your eyes say all the truth about you

No wonder, when you look here and there
You are hiding the things from the world or maybe
You are hiding yourself.

I like it when you show confidence **eye to eye**
As you possess no lies
Your eyes sparkle out of interest and excitement
It trembles with tears
And it blushes out in love too

No wonder eyes are gateway to heaven
Because I can see different galaxies at one sight
When I look through it, I realize
They all are same, made of stardust and some cosmic light.

8. Spiritual or not?

I am spiritual—
But don't confuse it with being religious.
Religion may be a path to walk,
But the destination remains the same.
I believe in spirits.
I believe in souls.
In past lives
And life after death.

But most of all,
I believe in the life I'm living now—
A perfect mix of sweetness, tang, and sorrow,
All stirred into one fleeting moment.
I believe in supreme energies—
In the flowers blooming through spring's breath,
In the sun's soft warmth on a chilly winter morning,
In the earthy scent of fresh rain on dry ground,
In the smile that finds its way back
After a stormy day.

I believe in the first bite after deep hunger,
In the quiet rhythm of bees, butterflies, squirrels, and birds.
I believe in the unspoken magic woven into all of it.

And that—

That is what I call spiritual.

9. Half love: half heart, how does it start?

He tells me I can only be loved whole heartedly
I wonder if he means what he said
If we can love with half heart too
or
Is he just saying it because he has no intention to fall in love
If what he says is true, so what kind of love could be done with a half heart?

It would be like praising the monsoon just by sitting in your room, windows and doors closed
Like complaining how lonely you are but avoiding people
or
maybe like calling yourself environmentalist without doing any contribution for its betterment

My whole life, love has been poured whole heartedly
And I don't know the other way round
It is either your whole heart for someone or none of it
I am curious to know if half of it can do justice
To something so powerful and above
Even if that happens, do we still call it love?

10. Wildflowers: A persuasion for love

I see how everyone gives roses, daisies, lilies
And other fancy flowers as greetings
But I would bring you wild flowers in our future meetings
To many, it may seem ordinary
But I find them beautiful and necessary

They will remind you of the beauty of the insignificant things
Things we don't pay much attention to
Just like how we neglect those tiny wild flowers in the valley at the sideways
They bloom making whole space heaven for many days

They will remind you to be brave and enough
Even if the weather gets tough
No matter the place these are rooted too,
they grow and glow with or without anyone
They do not require your appreciation to become
What they are or do what they do,
they bloom magnificently
That's the beauty they carry as a host
And that's the beauty I admire the most

So, I will bring you wild flowers to remind you that
Uncertainty is sometimes beautiful.

11. Beauty: an illusion or a state?

Beauty has different definition for different people
To some it is just physical features
To some its extraordinary places
While others see beauty in materialistic things
There are few who see beauty beyond eyes
Some find this beauty in small little things and rejoice

I think it lies everywhere,
How an ordinary thing can become beautiful to one
While others see nothing
It is a state of heart,
Someone with beautiful heart will always find
Beauty in places no one could ever imagine.

Those not finding it are the ones living in illusion
And deny all the beautiful possibilities.
this world can offer.

12. Magic: A lost tale

I see small children talking freely—
Of mermaids, unicorns, aliens, and spirits,
Their worlds bursting with color and wonder.

And I wonder—when do we lose that?
Where does all that faith go as we grow?
Imagination, dreams, and wild aspirations
Seem to fade with each passing year.

Adults say, "Magic isn't real,"
But I don't want to believe them.
I don't want to give up on the joy of wondering,
On the stories that lit up my soul.
I don't want that little girl I once was
To meet her future self and feel let down—
To find her dimmed, her spark gone cold.
I want to look her in the eye and say:
"Magic is real.
You are made of it.
Don't ever stop believing."

13. Am I really brave?

You called me brave and powerful
I wish you could have seen my trembling hands
Whenever I had to take the hard decision
My heart always pumped at its highest of highs
In the lowest lows of my life

But you, you only saw my smile when I was fighting
With the odds of life
You only saw me in the limelight
Things I showed to the world
And that made you envy me

But I, I have cried my nights just like a sweet sleep
With a hope that this would be the worst I will ever see
My eyes were as heavy as the soaked cotton balls
But I kept on smiling the very next day
I wish I could have thought of myself the same way as
you did.
So, I smiled and replied.
Thanks that comes naturally to me.

14. Freedom: does it tastes heavy?

You are truly enjoying the freedom
Said one of my friends
Do I? I wonder sometimes
The kind of freedom I crave is not mentioned in the vision
Of the people I surround myself with.
For them, the freedom is defined by the decisions I make
The money I earn or the work I do
But in my opinion that doesn't really makes me free
I am still bounded to these predefined notions of the world.

I want to be truly free from the thoughts that bow me down
I want to be physically rich enough to experience nature in its true self
I want to quench my thirst with the rivers around me and
want to travel to the tiniest villages of this world to meet the creatures never
praised enough.
And with every passing winter line, I want the freedom of time

But it feels like time is so less and I have so many miles
to go
Before I reach the last shore
I wish to taste this freedom In my life
I wish I could thrive.
And be really free.

15. Searching love: at wrong places.

Sometimes,
You search for love with all your heart—
In different places,
In different faces,
On quiet days,
In loud, fleeting embraces.
And then comes the disappointment—
Because you were chasing it
From someone too small to hold it,
Someone who doesn't even love themselves.
What else could you expect?

You start to question:
"Am I not good enough to be loved?"
But hear me—
You are more than enough.
Big enough to hold love,
Brave enough to give it.
You don't have to fight to find what's already yours.
It will come to you—gently, naturally.
Because love moves in circles.
It arrives without chaos or chase,
Without breaking you,

Without pain.

True love will never ask you to shrink.
It will not mold you into a mess.
If someone makes you feel less than you are—
They are not your person.
So stop feeding the flames of their ego.
You deserve the same love you give so freely.
You should never have to beg for it.
What is meant for you
Will find you—
Even across oceans,
Even through time.

Promise me this—
You won't trade your peace for a piece of someone.
You won't compromise your sanity.
Because love...
Love begins with you.
And remember—
Love keeps moving in circles.

16. Half love: half heart, how does it start?

He tells me I can only be loved whole heartedly
I wonder if he means what he said
If we can love with half heart too
Or
Is he just saying it because he has no intention to fall in
love
If what he says is true, so what kind of love could be
done with a half heart?

 It would be like praising the monsoon just by sitting in
your room, windows and doors closed
 Like complaining how lonely you are but avoiding
people
 Or maybe like calling yourself environmentalist without
doing any contribution for its betterment
 being a coward at the moments you were expected to be
brave.

 My whole life, love has been poured whole heartedly
 And I don't know the other way round
 It is either your whole heart for someone or none of it
 I am curious to know if half of it can do justice
 To something so powerful and above

Even if that happens, do we still call it love?
I doubt it will even last a while.

17. Sunrises & Sundowners

When I look at the sky, brushed with earthy hues,
It settles my chaos, makes me quietly whole.
There's peace in the beauty of things that don't last—
A fleeting moment, softly held.
No words were said, no wishes were spelled.

No wonder I have a thing for sunrises and sunsets—
I think maybe everyone does.
But when I watch them alone,
My heart feels a happiness words can't quite hold.
And that make me crave for them even more
assuring for calmer nights and better mornings.
I crave to witness these magical moments
from day to evenings and beginning to endings.

They feel like promises—
Of fresh beginnings, of gentle goodbyes.
Sometimes, somehow, they whisper:
It's all going to be okay.

18. The Blue I Don't Crave Anymore

If we could give colors to people—
To let them know how we feel,
I'd give you blue.
You've been my blue from the very start.
I fell for you
With all of my heart.
You made me feel peaceful—
And anxious—
All at once.
As if a quiet fear
Lingered between the lines.
And maybe...
Maybe I wasn't wrong to begin with.
Perhaps you were always the kind of blue
That doesn't stay forever—
But leaves a trace,
A hue that memory never erases.
Just a glimpse of you
Was what my eyes once craved the most.
But now—
You've become the blue
I no longer long for.

19. Old School Love

Call me old school,
But I believe in destiny.
Meeting you wasn't just chance—
It was written somewhere, meant to be.
Why else would I feel this sudden rush,
Like heaven wrapped in a moment's blush?

Call me old school,
But holding hands feels like magic to me.
That silent exchange, skin to skin—
Something only hearts can truly read.

Call me old school,
Because I'll write you letters instead of texts,
Pouring ink into feelings,
Where every word carries weight and depth.

Call me old school,
I crave the slow burn of love.
No rush, no race—
Let's take our time,
Unraveling each other one layer at a time,
Be it a whisper, a story, or a silent glance.

Call me old school,
Because I still believe in soulmates.
And I won't settle—
Not for anything less
Than the kind of love that feels like home.

20. Healing: with herb called life!

I'm healing—
But not in the way you think healing works.
You don't just wake up one day and *bam*,
You're the happiest version of yourself.
No, it's not that linear.
Its intensity swings—from soft like potatoes to sharp like lime,
While clinging to this fragile lifeline,
It takes its sweet, unpredictable time.

So yes,
I'm healing in bits and pieces,
Sometimes through people, sometimes through places.
Some days, I crash back to zero
And begin again.
Even when I don't feel worthy,
I'm there—for me.
Holding space,
Reminding myself that I've made it through before.
And I will again.
Some days, it's back and forth,
A dance with doubt,
A fight with hope.

Because healing isn't about winning—
It's about living.
Becoming.

In your own messy, beautiful way.
Even in your wildest dreams
And darkest nightmares—
You must heal.
Because without healing,
You don't thrive.
You just survive.
Let the emotions flow.
Don't bottle them, don't fake it.
This journey is not a sprint,
It's a lifelong process.
And always remember—
Acceptance is the key.
It's where healing begins.

21. Gestures of Love!

Gesture of love, or love language—call it what you may,
It always reminds me of things in a certain way.
I think of handwritten letters—
The ones I wrote,
The ones I received.
Pure emotion, sealed with time—
A piece of art so divine.
I've always been drawn to reading and writing,
To words that hold weight and meaning.

And for me,
A handwritten letter feels like gold.
No—*more precious than gold,*
More than diamonds—
A treasure of the soul.
So when I die,
I wish for just one thing:
For everyone who ever loved me
To write me one final letter—
By hand.
And to read it aloud at my farewell.
I want the room to echo with stories and smiles,
With our shared moments,
Our inside jokes,

Our quiet love.

Let my goodbye be a celebration—
Of a life fully lived,
And a heart that always believed
In the beauty of simple things.

22. In-Yun

The way your eyes meet mine
Takes me to a portal—
One that words can't quite define.
In that moment,
Seconds stretch into eternity.
As if we've known each other
In another world,
In another time—
A past life of infinity.

In-yun, maybe—
The red thread pulling me toward you.
So delicate,
Yet undeniably strong.
Your presence—
It fills my heart so completely,
I find myself whispering,
"I am whole again..."
Until we meet,
In the next life...

23. The kind of Women!

I don't want to be the woman who turns heads
When she walks down the road.
I want to be the one who settles
The chaos in your heart—
Just by having a conversation.

I don't want to awe you with possessions.
I want to challenge your thoughts,
Stir your obsessions,
Unravel the heavy lies
You were fed from the start—
And meet you halfway
In the matters of the heart.

I don't want to be the woman
You brag about to the world.
I want to be the one
You run to first—
To tell the smallest things,
Out loud and unfiltered.

24. Love with expiration date!

I wish loving you came with an expiration date.
The more I try to erase you from my mind,
The more space you seem to take.
But what about me?
Have I ever wandered into your most vulnerable
thoughts?
You give me mixed feelings—
Each one stirring doubts
That keep echoing through me.
So I keep wishing...
Wishing these feelings would fade
As time sways and seasons shift.
I don't want to be stuck
In this cycle of **unrequited love**.
My nights feel heavier,
The dark deeper—
With thoughts of you.

So yes,
I keep hoping love like this should have an expiration
date.
But then again...
Is it even possible?

25. Pink skies and you!

You are my pink.
The kind that feels like softness on the surface—
The kind that brings out the best in me.
You calm my chaos,
You lighten the heaviness
Of all my *why's* and *how's*.
Just like the pink skies,
You show up when I need you the most—
Soothing my soul
Whenever I feel lost.

And I want to show you off
To all my girlies—
Because my pink?
She's the best pink anyone could ever get.
I'm just so glad
That we met.

26. Tasteless man!

He asked me what he feels like to me.
I told him—
He's sweet.
But not just sweet—
Sometimes,
He's *tasteless*, too.
He laughed and asked,
"What does *tasteless* even mean?"

To me,
It's like food that depends on spices
To reveal its flavor.
He's like that—
A people person
Who draws flavor from the ones around him.
But that doesn't mean he lacks depth.
In fact, it's quite the art—
To feel everything at once,
Or nothing at all.
He doesn't always know what he feels
Until someone reflects it back to him.
And he sees that as a flaw.
But I don't.

I see it as a gift.
He can be any taste
At his own will.
He can shift and mold
In ways I never could.
And I hope—
One day he sees it too:
That being tasteless
Is just one of his many beautiful natures.
And secretly,
I wish I had that magic, too.

27. Worst days: A promise at hand!

How Would You Like to Be Comforted?
On your worst days,
How would you like to be comforted?
Would you want me to take your side—
Loud and proud?
Or just walk with you
To some quiet place,
Hand in hand?
I know life gets tough,
And the roads can turn rough.
But I'll be there for you,
No matter what.

So when the world flips upside down,
Or your smile fades into a frown—
Would you want to strike a quick happy deal?
Or maybe I could cook your favorite meal?
I'll show up when your days
Are shaded grey and white.
With flowers in hand
And sugar-free chocolate delights.
I know you're tired.
I know you avoid the sweet.

But I can still bring
Just the right amount of it—
Whenever you need.

So if the bad days hit you hard,
Like stone on skin—
My love,
You won't face them alone.
I'll be there.
Always.

28. Chasing the Waterfall

They told me to follow the ways of the world—
"Stay in line, or you'll be left unheard."
But little did they know, I never craved the easy way.
So I've decided—
I will chase the waterfall,
Not cling to rivers or lakes I've always known.
Yes, I might get bruised,
And yes, it may hurt—

But still, I'll go.
What if I find rainbows, full or half in arc?
Or, if I'm lucky, a chorus of them in the dark?
How would I ever know their hue,
Unless I dared this path—
One less traveled,
But deeply true?
Even if the stream roars fierce and steep,
I'll climb with wonder, not retreat.
I'll fill my cup with every fall,
And dance to nature's rhythm,
Never heard before at all.

I know I'll fall—again and again.
But isn't falling how we rise, how we begin?

To me, it's not a curse, but a boon.
Because I'm not giving up—
Not now. Not soon.

29. Small World

They say the world is vast—
You could spend a lifetime exploring
And still leave corners unseen.
Yet that one friend, living far away,
Can bring more comfort
Than a crowd close by.

Doesn't that make the world feel... small?
I know I won't reach every place—
But must I?
Does it even matter?
Why chase the impossible?
What use is a world too wide,
If it lies beyond my touch?

For me, the world is small—
It turns gently around a few dear souls,
The places I can reach,
The people I can hold,
The hobbies I can grow,
And the love I can give.

My world is made of moments—
Tiny memories stacked since childhood,

Little joys with grand delight.
And though my world is small,
My dreams are not.

They are big enough to stir the stars,
Yet close enough to touch.
I don't dream of a big world—
I live in a small world
With big, beautiful dreams.

30. Goodbyes

Goodbyes That Last Forever
Some goodbyes are harder than others—
for reasons we don't always understand.
I've seen thousands of farewells,
but a few...
a few shattered my world.
And it did crash down, for a while.
Yet we, as humans, are meant to endure—
endure till our last breath,
our final goodbye.

Some goodbyes, I chose myself.
Still, I wish some had never happened,
wish they were nothing more than
an awful, passing dream.
But in the shadows, memories linger—
strong enough to shake my soul.
Laughter,
tears,
echoes of moments we once shared.

With time, we learn to soften the ache.
Maybe that's why it doesn't hurt
like before.

So I carry these goodbyes
like a bittersweet song,
playing softly in the corners of my mind.

Though the pain may fade
like a fleeting dusk,
the love we shared—
a treasure I'll never unwind.

31. The Unusual Ones, Born Grown,

To the unusual men and women,
who became adults before their time—
carrying the burden of homes,
and the guilt etched on their parents' faces.
They work hard—so hard—
to fill a void the world left hollow.
They feel dejected,
as if the world itself was paranoid.

Yet they smile,
because they know how necessary it is.
They wear their scars like warriors,
and kindness on their sleeves.
These unusual men and women
become the pride of their parents.
They build their own legacy,
while helping others shape theirs.
They know how easy it is to blame,
but they choose to figure it out.
They know the world is harsh,
and yet,
they stand tall—
like the sun on a bright summer's day:

fiery and strong.

They choose to nurture the inner child
that was once silenced.
They understand that healing takes time.
And whatever they're doing now—it is wonderful,
even when doubt whispers,
"You could've done better."

They question authority,
challenge society,
because they know—
if they don't take a stand,
no one else ever will

32. A world without fields

They are building a world
with gadgets and gleaming machines,
paving roads of concrete dreams,
raising towers for future generations.
They are cutting trees—
trading green for grey,
clearing the earth
to make more room to stay.

But one day,
they'll see the cost was too high.
Technology won't give what they hoped to buy.
Their children will forget
how to speak with wonder,
how to run wild, in fields torn asunder.
Regret will bloom
where forests used to be.
And no screen or code
will quench their thirst or **set them free**.

33. Pookie souls!

Too soft for this world,
Were you told to be strong,
with a heart of steel?
Did those words make you question yourself?

Let's burst some bubbles:
This world needs *Pookie* souls,
or faith in humankind will be lost forever.
A heart is meant to be soft—
steel can never last.
You are a ray of hope in a world
turning grey with every passing day.

You bring waves of emotion to the shore,
and that makes you strong.
You shine with the softness within you,
making others feel equal and wise.
Your heart, a gentle force,
holds the power to heal and rebuild.
In a storm, it's the calm you bring,
the reminder **that love is always the thing.**

34. Autumn, My Muse!

The life itself no longer amazes me,
Yet the four seasons still carry its story.
I've always loved autumn—
The season of fall.

Everything turns dull, lifeless—
As if the earth is shedding its skin
To be born again.
To me, autumn brings hope—
A cooling breath after summer's blaze,
A time to open my wings
And soar into the clouds.

It offers a quiet promise:
That things will soften,
And the burdens I've carried for so long
Can be shed like old, torn clothes.
To me,
Autumn brings self-love.
Oh dear season,
I can't thank you enough.